YA   8/24/06 $30.95
956.7044   0-8368-7296-5
DOA
Doak, Robin
Conflicts in Iraq and Afghanistan

WARS THAT CHANGED AMERICAN HISTORY

Conflicts in Iraq and Afghanistan

Robin Doak

WORLD ALMANAC® LIBRARY

Please visit our Web site at: www.garethstevens.com
For a free color catalog describing World Almanac® Library's list of high-quality books
and multimedia programs, call 1-800-848-2928 (USA) or 1-800-387-3178 (Canada).
World Almanac® Library's fax: (414) 332-3567

Library of Congress Catalog-in-Publication Data

Doak, Robin S. (Robin Santos), 1963-
    Conflicts in Iraq and Afghanistan / by Robin Doak. — North American ed.
        p. cm. — (Wars that changed American history)
    Includes bibliographical references and index.
    ISBN-10: 0-8368-7296-7 – ISBN-13: 978-0-8368-7296-5 (lib. bdg.)
    ISBN-10: 0-8368-7305-X – ISBN-13: 978-0-8368-7305-4 (softcover)
    1. War on Terrorism, 2001—Juvenile literature. 2. Afghan War, 2001—Juvenile literature.
    3. Iraq War, 2003—Juvenile literature. 4. United States—Politics and government—2001-
    I. Title. II. Series.
    HV6431.D585 2007
    956.7044—dc22   2006011594

First published in 2007 by
World Almanac® Library
A Member of the WRC Media Family of Companies
330 West Olive Street, Suite 100
Milwaukee, WI 53212 USA

Copyright © 2007 by World Almanac® Library.

A Creative Media Applications, Inc. Production
Design and Production: Alan Barnett, Inc.
Editor: Susan Madoff
Copy Editor: Laurie Lieb
Proofreader: Laurie Lieb and Donna Drybread
Indexer: Nara Wood
World Almanac® Library editorial direction: Mark J. Sachner
World Almanac® Library editor: Alan Wachtel
World Almanac® Library art direction: Tammy West
World Almanac® Library production: Jessica Morris

Picture credits: Associated Press: Cover photo, pages 5, 8, 10, 11, 12, 14, 16, 19, 21, 22, 23, 24, 27, 28, 30, 33, 34, 35, 39, 40, 43; Landov: page 15; maps courtesy of Ortelius Design

Printed in the United States of America

1 2 3 4 5 6 7 8 9 10 09 08 07 06

Table of Contents

Cover: U.S. Marines walk past a mosque in Hit, Iraq, 125 miles (200 kilometers) west of Baghdad, in June 2005. The troops are part of Operation Sword, an offensive to crush insurgents in western Iraq.

From the time when America declared its independence in the 1700s to the present, every war in which Americans have fought has been a turning point in the nation's history. All of the major wars of American history have been bloody, and all of them have brought tragic loss of life. Some of them have been credited with great results, while others partly or entirely failed to achieve their goals. Some of them were widely supported; others were controversial and exposed deep divisions within the American people. None will ever be forgotten.

The American Revolution created a new type of nation based on the idea that the government should serve the people. As a result of the Mexican-American War, the young country expanded dramatically. Controversy over slavery in the new territory stoked the broader controversy between Northern and Southern states over the slavery issue and powers of state governments versus the federal government. When the slave states seceded, President Abraham Lincoln led the Union into a war against the Confederacy—the Civil War—that reunited a divided nation and ended slavery.

▼ Wars have shaped the history of the United States of America since the nation was founded in 1776. Conflict in this millennium continues to alter the decisions the government makes and the role the United States plays on the world stage.

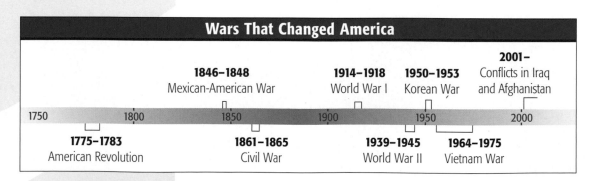

Wars That Changed America

		1846–1848 Mexican-American War	**1914–1918** World War I	**1950–1953** Korean War	**2001–** Conflicts in Iraq and Afghanistan
1750	1800	1850	1900	1950	2000
	1775–1783 American Revolution	**1861–1865** Civil War	**1939–1945** World War II	**1964–1975** Vietnam War	

The roles that the United States played in World War I and World War II helped transform the country into a major world power. In both these wars, the entry of the United States helped turn the tide of the war.

Later in the twentieth century, the United States engaged in a Cold War rivalry with the Soviet Union. During this time, the United States fought two wars to prevent the spread of communism. The Korean War essentially ended in a stalemate, and after years of combat in the Vietnam War, the United States withdrew. Both claimed great numbers of American lives, and following its defeat in Vietnam, the United States became more cautious in its use of military force.

This volume of *Wars that Changed American History* examines the most recent wars fought by the United States. Conflict between the United States and Iraq began in 1990 when the United States led an international coalition to drive Iraq's invading forces out of Kuwait. While relations between the United States and Iraq remained hostile, a new type of enemy carried out the first foreign attack on American soil in over 200 years. The United States responded by attacking Afghanistan, the country harboring the terrorist group that attacked it. Less than two years later, the United States led a controversial war to topple Saddam Hussein from power in Iraq.

▲ *Speaking aboard the aircraft carrier USS* Abraham Lincoln *in May 2003, President George W. Bush declared the end of "major combat operations" in Iraq. The statement, combined with a banner reading "Mission Accomplished" behind the president as he spoke, suggested to some that Bush was saying that the war was over. As fighting in Iraq continued – and as American casualties grew – critics of Bush began to question his abilities as a leader and his understanding of the difficulties facing Iraq.*

CHAPTER 1

The Persian Gulf War

For decades, the Middle East has been an international hot spot, a place of conflict, **turmoil**, and bloodshed. Fighting between nations as well as civil wars within some countries in the region has threatened world peace since the end of World War II. Although the **United Nations (UN)** and superpowers such as the United States have tried to broker peace agreements in the region, these efforts have been mixed—and often resented.

In 1979, Saddam Hussein came to power in Iraq. Saddam controlled the country with an iron fist, jailing or killing those who opposed his rule. He also invaded the neighboring country Iran, starting a bloody war that lasted eight years and resulted in the deaths of 500,000 people from both countries.

▼ *This map of the Middle East illustrates Iraq's location bordering Syria, Iran, Kuwait, Saudi Arabia, Jordan, and the Persian Gulf.*

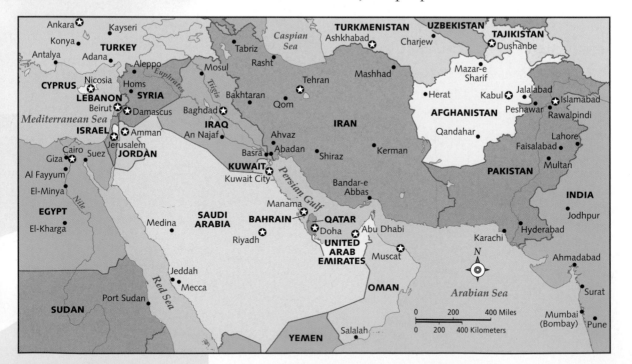

During the war, Saddam used chemical weapons against Iranian soldiers and **Kurdish** people in northern Iraq. The Kurds supported Iran.

In 1990, Saddam turned his attention to another neighbor, the tiny country of Kuwait. On August 2, Iraqi troops invaded Kuwait. Saddam wanted control of the small nation's profitable oil fields. He declared that Kuwait was now part of Iraq. He also moved troops to Kuwait's border with Saudi Arabia. Saudi Arabia feared it was the next target.

The World Reacts

Iraq's hostile invasion prompted an outcry around the world. Days after the invasion, the UN condemned Saddam's actions. The UN demanded the immediate and unconditional withdrawal of Iraqi troops from Kuwait.

At the same time, the United States began **deploying** troops to Saudi Arabia. The deployment was known as Operation Desert Shield. The presence of U.S. troops in the oil-rich nation was meant both to protect Saudi Arabia from an invasion by Iraq and to scare Saddam into withdrawing from Kuwait.

During Operation Desert Shield, President George H. W. Bush authorized military **reservists** to be called up for action. By November 1990, about 540,000 U.S. troops were in the Persian Gulf and ready for action. Although the United States sent the bulk of troops and supplies, the deployment was a **multinational** mission. In all, thirty-nine nations contributed to the international **coalition** of forces.

Once the multinational force was in place in Saudi Arabia, the UN gave Saddam an ultimatum: Leave Kuwait by January 15 or suffer the consequences. Saddam refused to withdraw his troops from Iraq's new "province."

Fast Fact

Sandwiched between Iraq and Saudi Arabia, the hot, desert nation of Kuwait is small in size but big in resources. The country, located in the northwestern corner of the Persian Gulf, is just slightly larger than the state of Connecticut. It is the location, however, of about one-tenth of the world's known oil reserves. In the 1980s, Kuwait supported Iraq in its war against Iran.

On January 17, 1991, the multinational coalition, or alliance, began waging war on Iraq. The attack was placed under the command of U.S. general Norman Schwarzkopf. The first part of the assault was a series of **aerial** bombings on selected targets in both Iraq and Kuwait. This attack was called Operation Desert Storm.

Freeing Kuwait

During the early days of the operation, U.S. and coalition fighter planes took off on thousands of combat missions, bombing targets in and around Baghdad, the capital of Iraq. Bombs destroyed Iraqi government buildings, weapons stockpiles, communications towers, oil wells, bridges, and roads. Later attacks targeted Iraqi troops in and near Kuwait. Iraq retaliated by launching missile attacks on Saudi Arabia and Israel. (Although Israel was not involved in the fighting, it is a major ally of the United States in the Middle East.)

After five weeks of devastating aerial assaults, Saddam refused to surrender. Ground troops then prepared for the second part of the attack on Iraq, called Operation Desert Sabre. On February 23, coalition troops entered Kuwait from Saudi Arabia. Their goal was to **liberate** the country. Along the way, they battled and easily defeated Iraqi troops, with few casualties among their own forces.

As coalition troops moved across the desert toward Kuwait's capital, Kuwait City, Iraqi troops fled. As they retreated, they retaliated by looting homes and

▼ *Kuwaiti shop owner Muhammad Carsym stands amid the rubble of his destroyed jewelry store in Kuwait City's business district in March 1991. The entire shopping district was torn apart and looted in the Persian Gulf War.*

Conflicts in Iraq and Afghanistan

buildings and setting hundreds of Kuwait's oil wells on fire. By February 27, Kuwait City was secure, and the country was declared liberated. Driving out Iraq's forces had taken just one hundred hours.

Shortly after, President Bush called for a cease-fire. At this time, coalition leaders decided to end the war and not attempt to remove Saddam and his remaining Republican Guard military troops from power.

A peace agreement between coalition forces and Iraq, accepted by Saddam on April 6, 1991, required the Iraqis to pay for war damages in Kuwait and destroy all **weapons of mass destruction** (WMDs) and other arms. Unless Iraq complied with the terms of the agreement, the UN would continue **economic sanctions** that had first been imposed upon Iraq in August 1990, shortly after Iraq invaded Kuwait.

The End of a War

With a peace agreement in place, U.S. troops began leaving the Persian Gulf. The Persian Gulf War had lasted little more than six weeks. Nearly three hundred U.S. soldiers died and more than 450 were wounded. The war cost the United States more than $61 billion, much of which was paid back by other nations. Iraqis had suffered even worse casualties. Although exact statistics do not exist, one military analyst estimated that as many as sixty-three hundred Iraqi soldiers were killed. About three thousand civilians also died during the war. About seventy thousand Iraqis, both soldiers and civilians, were left homeless.

After returning from Iraq, many Gulf War veterans from the United States, Great Britain, and other nations suffered from a group of medical problems that some doctors labeled "**Gulf War syndrome**." Physical ailments associated with this syndrome include fatigue, aches and pains, headaches, and skin

Operation Desert Fox

On December 16, 1998, President Bill Clinton announced that the United States had once again begun bombing selected targets in Iraq. The goal of the mission, called Operation Desert Fox, was to destroy Saddam's ability to make weapons of mass destruction. More than thirty thousand U.S. troops took part in the attack, which included a number of air strikes launched from U.S. destroyers and air bases. Over a four-day period, U.S. aircraft dropped bombs on one hundred targets, including suspected weapons factories and Republican Guard headquarters. There were no U.S. fatalities during the strikes.

▲ A 1990 photo shows U.S. soldiers in Saudi Arabia wearing gas masks as they train to protect themselves against chemical weapons attacks in anticipation of deployment in Operation Desert Shield.

rashes. Mental ailments included stress, inability to concentrate, and depression.

Medical experts are not sure what causes Gulf War syndrome. Some believe that exposure to nerve gas and other chemical weapons in Iraq may be responsible for the illness. Others believe that shots given to soldiers to protect them from diseases and chemical weapons may have contributed to the illness. Yet others believe that the syndrome is stress-related. Some government agencies even reject the idea that there is a unique Gulf War syndrome that affects veterans. Most experts agree that the exact cause of these ailments among Gulf War veterans will never be known.

Although the Persian Gulf War ended, the struggles between Saddam and the rest of the world had only just begun. In the coming years, Saddam would thwart the efforts of UN weapons inspectors to make sure that Iraq was complying with the terms of the peace agreement. In 1996, Iraqi troops attacked a Kurdish town in northern Iraq. The Kurds are a people whose homeland includes areas in Iraq, Syria, Turkey, Armenia, and Iran. In the years after the Gulf War, the efforts of Iraqi Kurds to establish self-government resulted in attacks on their towns and cities by Saddam's army. After the 1996 hostilities, the United States again launched missile strikes against Iraqi military targets. The attack was known as Operation Desert Strike. Economic sanctions against Iraq continued to affect the people in the country.

Conflicts in Iraq and Afghanistan

CHAPTER 2

Terrorism at Home and Abroad

In the final years of the twentieth century, certain groups began waging an undeclared war against the United States through **terrorism**. Terrorism has been used as a tool by individuals and groups for centuries. According to some experts, terrorism is "the poor man's weapon." The use of such terrorist methods as suicide bombings, kidnappings, and shootings temporarily gives small radical groups the power to inflict pain and terror upon larger groups. Throughout the 1990s, random violent terrorist acts warned Americans traveling in other parts of the world—especially the Middle East—that they could be targets in this new type of war.

Today, many terrorists are extremist or radical **Muslims**. Of course, not all Muslims are terrorists. In fact, many scholars say that terrorism and suicide bombings are against the principles of **Islam**. According to most Islamic scholars, *jihad*, the Islamic term meaning "holy war" does not include acts of terrorism. As a result of the actions of **Islamist radicals**, however, many peace-loving Muslims in the United States and

▼ *New York City police officers investigate the damage from a bomb detonated inside the World Trade Center in February 1993 by an Islamic fundamentalist group. Six people were killed and more than one thousand injured in the attack, foreshadowing the devastation of the 2001 attacks at the same site.*

other nations have suffered from prejudice and harassment in recent years.

Many Americans wonder why the Islamist terrorists hate the United States. Some experts point to U.S. support of Israel, a Jewish state that is surrounded by Muslim nations. These nations resented the division of Jerusalem, a holy city for Muslims, Jews, and Christians. Others believe that U.S. military and economic interference in the Persian Gulf has turned the Muslim world against the United States. In the past, for example, U.S. officials have supported corrupt, repressive governments in the Middle East. In addition, the economic sanctions against Iraq, meant to weaken Saddam Hussein's government, most seriously affected the common people of Iraq. The sanctions included a boycott on almost all international trade with the nation. The only items allowed into the country were food for humanitarian purposes and medicines. However, the sanctions resulted in many Iraqis, especially children, suffering from malnutrition and sickness; they had little effect on Saddam and his followers.

▼ Islamic rebels fighting off the Soviets rest in the Kunar province of Afghanistan in May 1980. Many of these rebels, who believed they were fighting a holy war against the Soviets, formed the backbone of al-Qaeda cells that developed outside of Afghanistan in the decade following the Soviet occupation.

Al-Qaeda

Many of today's terrorist groups are linked in larger terrorist **networks** that pursue a common goal. These larger terrorist organizations are often divided into **cells,** smaller units that operate independently, with one cell often unaware of what the others are doing.

One of the most notorious terrorist networks is al-Qaeda,

which takes its name from the Arabic words meaning "the foundation" or "the military base." The group that would become al-Qaeda was formed in 1988 by Muslim extremists in Afghanistan. Originally founded to help Muslims expel Soviet forces from the country, it evolved into an organization whose goal was to oppose what its leaders see as corrupt Islamic governments and nations that interfered in the affairs of the Muslim world. One of al-Qaeda's chief aims was to establish one Islamic government throughout the Middle East. By 2001, it was said to include terrorist groups in more than seventy countries.

Al-Qaeda is headed by Saudi Arabian millionaire Osama bin Laden. His hatred of the United States grew strong after the Persian Gulf War and the presence of U.S. troops in Saudi Arabia. He believes that the presence of U.S. troops—the vast majority of whom are not Muslim—is offensive in the Islamic world.

Attack on the United States

In early 1993, terrorists targeted the World Trade Center in New York City. Since the early 1970s, the trade center's two, 110-story towers had topped New York City's skyline, serving as a center for many international and American businesses. For Americans and foreigners alike, the Twin Towers of the World Trade Center, among the tallest buildings in the world, were a symbol of American success and power.

On February 26, terrorists parked a rented van filled with explosives in the parking garage beneath the twin buildings. The resulting explosion left six people dead and about one thousand injured. A Pakistani man named Ramzi Yousef was later arrested for masterminding the attack. Yousef had ties to al-Qaeda and was influenced by an extremist Muslim preacher living

The Taliban

Beginning in 1996, al-Qaeda was protected by the Taliban, a radical Islamic group that seized control of Afghanistan's government in the mid-1990s. The Taliban are an Afghani Islamist organization that believed in strictly following Islamic law. After they took control of Afghanistan, the Taliban insisted that Afghanis follow rigid social rules. Women, for example, were no longer allowed to work outside the home or attend school. Television, sports, music, and the Internet were forbidden. Even minor lawbreakers were harshly punished. Few governments recognized the Taliban as Afghanistan's legal government.

in New York. In 1997, he was convicted and sentenced to life in prison without parole.

Saddam Hussein also sponsored acts of terror. Two months after the World Trade Center bombing, for example, Iraqi agents planned to assassinate former president George Bush while he was visiting Kuwait. Although the plan was discovered and the assassination prevented, President Clinton retaliated by launching a missile attack on Iraq in June 1993.

Throughout the mid-1990s, terrorist groups, unhappy with the continued U.S. military presence in the Middle East, continued their attacks on U.S. targets. In November 1995, terrorists attacked a military installation in Riyadh, Saudi Arabia. Seven people were killed, including five Americans. Seven months later, terrorists bombed the Khobar Towers near Dhahran, Saudi Arabia. The high-rise apartment complex served as a home to U.S. military personnel. Nineteen people were killed, and hundreds were wounded.

▲ Nineteen U.S. servicemen based in the Khobar Towers in Saudi Arabia (pictured here) were killed in June 1996 when a truck bomb ripped through the military facility, located at Abdul Aziz Air Base.

Bin Laden Emerges

In September 1996, Osama bin Laden issued a **fatwa** declaring war on American citizens in Saudi Arabia. Two years later, he issued a second fatwa calling for all Muslims to "kill the Americans and their allies, civilians and military . . . in any country in which it is possible to do so." Most Muslims rejected this call to arms. They questioned whether bin Laden, who is not a Muslim cleric, had any authority to issue such a decree and whether other Muslims had any responsibility to obey it.

Conflicts in Iraq and Afghanistan

On August 7, 1998, the American embassy buildings in Kenya and Tanzania, both in East Africa, were bombed by terrorists in local al-Qaeda cells. The embassies were completely destroyed, and the bombs killed more than 230 people. Twelve of the dead were Americans. Five thousand people were wounded in the attacks. Although people around the world were shocked by the bombings, al-Qaeda believed that none of those killed were innocent bystanders. Like other terrorist organizations that target civilians, the group believed that anyone who cooperated or worked with the enemy is also an enemy.

After four months of investigation, bin Laden and nineteen others were charged by the United States in the attacks. Afghan officials, however, refused to turn the terrorist leader over for trial. President Clinton then authorized missile attacks on al-Qaeda training camps in Afghanistan. The air strikes, beginning on December 16, 1998, lasted for four days, but they failed to kill bin Laden.

In 2000, al-Qaeda was again linked to another deadly attack on Americans. This time, terrorists struck in the Middle Eastern country of Yemen. On October 12, suicide bombers drove a small motorboat filled with explosives into the USS *Cole*, a U.S. Navy destroyer on duty in the port of Aden. Seventeen sailors were killed in the blast, and thirty-nine more were wounded.

At this time, the most spectacular and bloody of all terrorist attacks was in the works. With the financial support of bin Laden, a group of al-Qaeda terrorists were training to fight, kill, and fly planes. In less than a year's time, they would be ready. These terrorist acts would lead the United States into a war far from home.

Osama bin Laden

Born into a wealthy Saudi Arabian family in 1957, Osama bin Laden, (*above*), was thirteen years old, when his father died, leaving him millions of dollars. As he grew older, the devout Muslim turned to extreme forms of Islam. Bin Laden set as his goal the re-creation of a Muslim empire throughout the Middle East, one that would strictly follow Muhammad's teachings.

In 1980, bin Laden began his career in terror by aiding Muslims fighting against invading Soviet troops in Afghanistan. He believed that non-Muslims—whether Soviet or American—had no business interfering in Islamic lands. Ten years later, after the United States set up bases in Saudi Arabia to pre-pare for Operation Desert Storm, bin Laden began tar-geting Americans and U.S. holdings. Today, bin Laden is still at large—and still at the top of the Most Wanted list of the Federal Bureau of Investigaton (FBI).

CHAPTER 3

September 11 and Its Aftermath

▼ *The South Tower of the World Trade Center in New York City collapses amid smoke billowing from both towers after hijackers crashed airplanes into them on September 11, 2001. The 110-story towers were destroyed in the attack, which killed almost three thousand people.*

September 11, 2001, was a warm, sunny day. For people heading to work in New York City, it was business as usual. The day quickly turned into a nightmare, however, when nineteen terrorists hijacked four airplanes on the East Coast of the United States. With the terrorists at the controls, each plane became a flying bomb. The undeclared war against the United States had, again, been brought to American soil. The coming events would forever change the way Americans thought about terrorism and the nature of war.

At 8:46 A.M., American Airlines Flight 11 smashed into the North Tower of the World Trade Center. The Boeing 767, loaded with 16,000 pounds (7,264 kilograms) of jet fuel, exploded upon impact, immediately killing the hijackers, the ninety-two passengers and crew members aboard the plane, and people at the impact site. The fire from the explosion set the building on fire.

People who witnessed the crash were stunned. Most believed that the crash was a terrible accident. Less than twenty minutes later, however, New Yorkers watched in horror as a second plane, United Airlines Flight 175, flew into the World Trade Center's South Tower. The plane carried sixty-five passengers and crew members.

It was now clear that the United States was under attack. New York's airports, tunnels, and bridges were quickly shut down. The Federal Aviation Administration (FAA) shut down all the airports across the nation. Any plane that was currently in flight was ordered to land at the nearest airport. But it was already too late. Terrorists had control of two more planes that were still in the air.

The Attacks Continue

The hijackers' attack on New York City was only half of the plan. At 9:37 A.M., American Airlines Flight 77 crashed into the Pentagon in Washington, D.C. The Pentagon is the headquarters of the U.S. military, and it is a symbol of the country's military might. The crash killed a total of 184 people on the ground and in the plane.

United Airlines Flight 93 was the fourth and final plane to be hijacked. Four terrorists broke into the cockpit and overpowered the plane's flight crew. Then they transmitted a chilling message that was overheard by air traffic controllers on the ground: "Ladies and gentlemen: Here the captain, please sit down keep remaining seating. We have a bomb on board. So sit." Armed with the knowledge that a fourth hijacked plane was headed toward Washington D.C., people acted quickly. Officials evacuated the White House, the U.S. Capitol (where U.S. Congress meets), and other federal buildings. Flight 93, however, never made it to Washington, D.C. At 10:03, the plane crashed into a field in Pennsylvania.

Predicting a Terrorist Attack

The September 11 terrorist attacks were not a complete shock for a very small group of Americans. In February 2001, Central **Intelligence** Agency (CIA) director George Tenet warned the U.S. Senate that al-Qaeda was a serious threat to American security. In a report published a month later, a committee on national security warned, "Americans will likely die on American soil, possibly in large numbers." This warning, however, was largely ignored by both politicians and the media.

After terrorists took control of the plane, many passengers on Flight 93 used mobile phones to call friends and loved ones. During their conversations, they learned that three other planes had been deliberately crashed into buildings. They decided to take action to prevent the terrorists from doing the same with Flight 93. A group of passengers and flight attendants stormed the cockpit and stopped the terrorists from carrying out their deadly plan of destruction.

The crash of Flight 93 was a tragedy that cost more than 40 innocent people their lives. A much larger disaster, however, was averted. Later, investigators stated that the hijackers intended to steer the plane into the White House or the U.S. Capitol.

The Towers Collapse

At the same time that passengers on Flight 93 were battling for control of the plane, Americans and people around the world watched on television as the unthinkable disaster worsened. Just before 10:00 A.M., the South Tower began to shudder, and then it crashed to the ground. Thirty minutes later, the North Tower collapsed.

About 2,750 people were killed when the two towers fell. More than four hundred of those killed were emergency workers, firefighters, and police officers who entered the buildings to aid and rescue others. In all, nearly three thousand people died during the terrorist attacks on September 11.

Dealing with a Crisis

When the attacks on the World Trade Center began, President George W. Bush was in a classroom in Sarasota, Florida, reading to schoolchildren. After

the second crash, he was flown first to Louisiana, then to a safe site in Nebraska. By 7:00 P.M., President Bush had returned to the White House. Later in the evening, he addressed Americans on television. "America has stood down enemies before, and we will do so this time," Bush told viewers. "None of us will ever forget this day. Yet, we go forward to defend freedom and all that is good and just in our world."

In New York and Washington, D.C., firefighters and volunteers continued to comb frantically through the wreckage of the crash sites, looking for survivors. In New York, four people were miraculously pulled from beneath the rubble. Hope for finding others alive soon faded, however, and the nation turned to the task of mourning the dead and cleaning up the more than 1.5 million tons (1.36 million metric tons) of **debris**.

In the days following the tragedy, information about the terrorists and their plans was slowly revealed. For example, the day after the attacks, it was learned that several of the terrorists had

Rebuilding the World Trade Center Site

Soon after 9/11, New Yorkers began debating what should be done at what had come to be called Ground Zero, the site where the Twin Towers once stood. Some people felt that two new towers should be built, higher and stronger than the originals. Others felt the site should be left empty in memory of those who lost their lives in the terrorist attacks.

Eventually a plan was selected: four new towers surrounding a large memorial to the victims of 9/11. The tallest tower will be 1,776 feet (542 meters) tall. On July 4, 2004, the first new building's cornerstone was laid. The total area, which is the size of fifteen football fields, will include offices, stores, cultural buildings, and a transportation hub.

attended flight schools in the United States to learn to fly jumbo jets. Less than a week after the attack, President Bush announced that the mastermind behind the plan was most likely Osama bin Laden.

The 9/11 Commission

After September 11, many people wondered if the terrorist attacks could have been prevented. To answer this question, Congress formed the 9/11 Commission in November 2002. The commission's goals were to record the events of September 11, 2001, and to recommend actions to keep the United States safe from future terrorist attacks.

In the coming months, the commission interviewed hundreds of people and held public hearings to gather testimony. Commission members began speaking out, saying that the terrorist attacks were, in fact, preventable. In December 2003, commission chair Thomas Keane told reporters, "This was not something that had to happen."

The commission published its findings in July 2004. The 585-page report pointed out intelligence lapses and a failure on the part of the FBI and the CIA to share information on known terrorists and their actions. The FAA was also faulted for failing to establish adequate security measures that might have thwarted the terrorists. Additionally, according to the commission, before the attack U.S. officials overlooked falsified visas and doctored passports belonging to the hijackers. The report also stated that even before 9/11, government officials had warned that bin Laden was a serious and immediate threat to the United States. Few people in power believed, however, that al-Qaeda was capable of carrying out a major attack on U.S. soil. The 9/11 Commission recommended that several new posts be created within the federal government to oversee federal intelligence agencies.

Conflicts in Iraq and Afghanistan

CHAPTER 4

The War in Afghanistan

After the September 11 attacks, Americans debated what the United States should do next. Many were in favor of an immediate attack on Afghanistan, the country harboring Osama bin Laden. Others felt that any war at this time would be a mistake.

On September 20, President Bush addressed Congress and the nation. In his speech, Bush demanded that the Taliban government in Afghanistan surrender Osama bin Laden and other al-Qaeda leaders to the United States. He also discussed the new kind of war, a war on terrorism, that the nation planned to wage against terrorists around the world:

▲ President Bush, addressing a joint session of Congress on September 20, 2001, holds up the badge of New York Port Authority police officer George Howard, who died while trying to save others in the World Trade Center attack earlier in the month.

> Americans should not expect one battle, but a lengthy campaign, unlike any other we have ever seen. It may include dramatic strikes, visible on TV, and covert operations, secret even in success. We will starve terrorists of funding, turn them one against another, drive them from place to place, until there is no refuge or no rest. And we will pursue nations that provide aid or safe haven to terrorism. Every nation, in every region, now has a decision to make. Either you are with us, or you are with the terrorists.

Bush also implied that some sort of military response was in the works. He said, "Our grief has turned to anger and anger to resolution. Whether we bring our enemies to justice or bring justice to our enemies, justice will be done." Congress had already authorized the president to use force to punish the terrorists behind the September 11 hijackings. To prepare for such an attack, thousands of military reservists were placed on active duty.

The Taliban refused to immediately hand over bin Laden. Instead, they asked for proof that the Saudi was behind the attacks. On October 7, 2001, the United States attacked Afghanistan. The short-term goal of Operation Enduring Freedom, as the assault was called, was the destruction of terrorist training camps and the capture of al-Qaeda members. A longer-term goal was to put a complete end to terrorism within the country of Afghanistan. Most Americans supported the invasion of Afghanistan. A poll taken in September

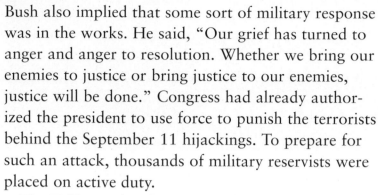

▼ A reward offered for information leading to the capture of Osama bin Laden and his top lieutenant in al-Qaeda, Ayman al-Zawahri, was intended to spur Afghans to aid in the search for the terrorists in the rugged mountain caves where they were believed to be hiding at the time.

showed that 82 percent favored taking military action "to retaliate against whoever is responsible for the terrorist attacks." Americans knew that the Taliban government was harboring the man believed to be behind the terrible events of September 11.

Operation Enduring Freedom began with aerial assaults on Taliban targets. American and British warplanes dropped bombs on Taliban bases, training camps, and suspected bin Laden hideouts throughout the country. These massive air strikes destroyed radar installations, antiaircraft missiles, and airfields, effectively destroying the Taliban's ability to stop the air raids.

Conflicts in Iraq and Afghanistan

U.S. Special Forces began arriving in Afghanistan in mid-October, joining forces with anti-Taliban Afghan fighters known as the Northern Alliance. Many other nations around the world also sent soldiers and supplies. Together, the coalition troops captured several Afghan cities, including Kabul, the capital, on November 13. In the coming days, U.S. forces succeeded in over-running Kandahar, the Taliban's military center, and driving the Taliban and al-Qaeda out of power.

▲ In December 2001, U.S. Marines leave Camp Rhino in southern Afghanistan to patrol the region as part of Operation Enduring Freedom.

The war in Afghanistan marked an advance in military technology. Many military communications devices and weapons were new or much improved in 2001. The accuracy of missiles was far superior to what it had been ten years earlier, during the Persian Gulf War. As a result, fewer missiles were needed to destroy targets, and the amount of damage to non-targeted sites was greatly reduced. Unmanned aerial vehicles also proved important, providing constant **monitoring** of troops and targets.

In mid-December UN and Afghan leaders began the process of setting up a new Afghan government. Many U.S. troops remained in Afghanistan, searching the country's caves, mountains, and forests for al-Qaeda and Taliban leaders. Although some top leaders were captured, Osama bin Laden was not. He remained on the loose in early 2006, despite a $25 million reward for his capture offered by the U.S. Department of Justice.

Taking Prisoners

During Operation Enduring Freedom, U.S. forces detained many members of al-Qaeda. By questioning these terrorists, U.S. intelligence officials hoped to learn about al-Qaeda and its operations.

Hundreds of captured prisoners, both al-Qaeda and Taliban, were flown to the U.S. naval base in Guantánamo Bay, Cuba. Here, the prisoners were held without being charged with any crime. They were closely questioned about the workings of al-Qaeda. Some detainees later said that they had been treated inhumanely, beaten, or tortured.

Many people were outraged by what they believed was the cruel and illegal detention of the prisoners. These people believed that the United States was not following the rules of the Geneva Convention. This agreement, first signed by representatives of the United States and other countries in 1864, protects the rights of prisoners of war. President Bush responded by saying that terrorists do not fall under Geneva Convention guidelines. He also stated that the United States had the right to hold these men because they presented a threat to the country's security. Despite calls from the UN to close the base, Guantánamo remained open. In April 2006, the United States announced plans to release 141 of the nearly five hundred men still detained there.

Taken in Secret

In late 2005, stories about secret CIA overseas detention centers surfaced in the news. According to reports, some people of Arab descent who were suspected of being terrorists, were plucked off the streets in

Conflicts in Iraq and Afghanistan

Germany and Italy by the CIA. The reports said that these suspects were blindfolded and flown to secret destinations in several countries around the world to be questioned and imprisoned. Some who were later released claimed that they had been tortured.

People around the world were outraged by this treatment. Secretary of State Condoleezza Rice, however, justified the government's handling of the prisoners. "One of the difficult issues in this new kind of conflict is what to do with captured individuals who we know or believe to be terrorists," Rice said. "The captured terrorists of the 21st century do not fit easily into traditional systems of criminal or military justice, which were designed for different needs. We have to adapt."

Known CIA detention centers were located in Thailand, Afghanistan, and several Middle Eastern nations. Additionally, a human rights organization accused Poland and Romania of possibly hosting the secret prisons. In January 2006, a European Union (EU) investigation into secret U.S. detention centers in Europe found no indisputable evidence that such centers existed. The head of the probe, however, said that evidence suggested that suspected terrorists were picked up in the EU and flown to other parts of the world for questioning and torture.

Afghanistan Today

Afghanistan, ripped apart by war for decades, is slowly recovering. In 2004, the country held a successful presidential election; women were allowed to participate in the voting. The nation is gradually being put back together as roads, schools, hospitals, and other public works structures are built or repaired. The United States has played a key role, guiding Afghanistan's transition to democracy and

Top al-Qaeda Prisoners

Since the war on terror began, the United States has captured several top al-Qaeda operatives. Two of the most important terrorists in U.S. custody are Khalid Shaikh Muhammad and his aid, Ramzi Binalshibh. Both men are said, along with Osama bin Laden, to have masterminded the September 11 attacks. Binalshibh was the first to be captured. He was picked up in Pakistan in September 2002. Six months later, Muhammad was also captured in Pakistan. At some point after the men were captured, the U.S. government moved them to undisclosed locations. Human rights organizations believe that the prisoners are being held in isolation and tortured to gain information about past and future terrorist attacks.

The United States and bin Laden

During the time that the Soviet Union occupied Afghanistan (1979–1989), the United States secretly worked to help opposition forces overthrow the government there. The CIA provided training and financial support to an agency founded by Osama bin Laden to undermine the Soviet-controlled regime. This U.S. support was first funneled through a Pakistani government agency.

providing money and other aid to help the country rebuild. For example, the U.S. government has improved agriculture in Afghanistan by training farmers, repairing irrigation systems, and providing fertilizer and seeds for crops. Since the end of the war, the United States has spent millions of dollars to help Afghanistan recover.

Many problems, however, still exist. The Taliban continue to fight against Afghanistan's new government. At the beginning of 2006, Taliban leader Muhammad Omar publicly stated that his followers should continue fighting. Taliban-led suicide bombings, shootings, and other terrorist attacks have increased in recent years, especially in areas of the country that formerly supported the Taliban government.

So far, the war has been costly. Since October 2001, operations in Afghanistan have cost the United States about $47 billion. The war also took a human toll. More than 275 U.S. troops have been killed in Afghanistan; nearly a hundred of them died in 2005. As of March 2006, about nineteen thousand U.S. troops still remain in Afghanistan, although that number is expected to drop soon. A U.S. presence will continue to be felt in Afghanistan while the country rebuilds and works toward stability.

The war also signaled a change in President Bush's foreign policy. When he campaigned for office in 2000, Bush pledged to avoid the kind of **nation-building** that occurs when a powerful nation guides and assists the efforts of another country to restructure itself, often by occupying the weaker country. After the war in Afghanistan, U.S. foreign policy changed. Bush now believed that nation-building could help to keep the United States safe by setting up a stable democratic government in Afghanistan—and other nations.

Conflicts in Iraq and Afghanistan

CHAPTER 5

The War on Terrorism at Home

The September 11 attacks showed that a new kind of warfare, waged by terrorist fighters, could be brought onto U.S. soil from abroad. To fight this new war, Americans agreed that, in addition to capturing terrorists in Afghanistan, precautions needed to be taken to make the United States safer. After the attacks, the state and federal governments acted to protect nuclear power plants, water supply systems, and other sensitive sites. America's borders with Canada and Mexico were more carefully guarded, and the United States started cracking down on foreign citizens who overstayed their legal time in the country.

On September 18, 2001, Americans learned of a new threat to their safety: **anthrax**, a type of bacteria that causes a potentially fatal disease also known as anthrax. This bacteria can be used as a terrorist weapon because it is easily grown, can survive in many conditions, and is deadly even in small amounts.

Over a period of several weeks, seven letters containing anthrax **spores** were sent to government officials and media offices. Twenty-two

▼ Members of the U.S. Marine Corps' Chemical-Biological Incident Response Force (CBIRF) stand outside the Capitol in October 2001 as part of a government demonstration for the press illustrating how chemical contamination is investigated and cleaned. The instruction comes in the wake of building closings on Capitol Hill due to concerns about anthrax.

people who opened the letters and inhaled the deadly powder became infected. Five people died, including two U.S. postal workers. Investigators have been unable to identify who sent the anthrax-laced letters.

Anthrax isn't the only biochemical weapon that could be used against Americans. Other potential terrorist tools include the contagious smallpox virus, which Americans are no longer vaccinated against, and salmonella and E. coli, two bacteria that could be used to infect water or food supplies. Experts say, however, that chances of an attack with these agents are low.

Homeland Security

In October 2001, President Bush created the Office of Homeland Security. As the first chief of Homeland Security, Bush chose Pennsylvania governor Tom Ridge.

In March 2002, Ridge announced the Homeland Security Advisory System. The system uses color codes to warn Americans about the risk of a terrorist attack on any given day. Five colors warned of five different levels of threat— from green (low risk) to red (severe risk). The system also suggested safety steps to be taken for each level of risk.

In November 2002, the agency was reorganized into the Department of Homeland Security. Ridge continued to be in charge of the newly named department, which now included more than twenty other federal agencies, including the Federal Emergency Management Agency, Customs and Border Protection, Secret Service, and Coast Guard.

▼ This chart illustrates the five-level, color-coded terrorism warning system established by the Office of Homeland Security director Tom Ridge in 2002.

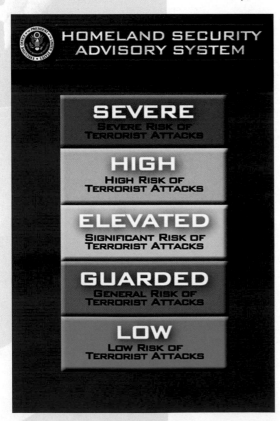

HOMELAND SECURITY
ADVISORY SYSTEM

SEVERE
SEVERE RISK OF
TERRORIST ATTACKS

HIGH
HIGH RISK OF
TERRORIST ATTACKS

ELEVATED
SIGNIFICANT RISK OF
TERRORIST ATTACKS

GUARDED
GENERAL RISK OF
TERRORIST ATTACKS

LOW
LOW RISK OF
TERRORIST ATTACKS

Conflicts in Iraq and Afghanistan

The Patriot Act

Another way the federal government hoped to keep Americans safe from terrorism was through the USA Patriot Act. The Patriot Act, passed by Congress in October 2001, gave the government and law enforcement agencies broad powers in finding and dealing with suspected terrorists. The law expanded the ability of such agencies, with a judge's approval, to conduct searches, keep tabs on people through library, bank, and medical records, and even detain people for long periods of time without stating a cause.

The law has sparked furious debate since it was passed. Some Americans complain that the Patriot Act takes away their right to privacy, a right that is highly prized and historically protected in the United States. Many Muslim Americans especially feel that there is an atmosphere of suspicion surrounding them. Some colleges have been asked to turn over data on Arab or Muslim students. For Arabs or Muslims visiting or studying in the United States, thousands have been questioned by government agencies in the years since the Patriot Act was passed.

One of the most controversial parts of the Patriot Act was a provision that allowed the FBI to obtain secret warrants to search a person's library records and bookstore purchases. It also allowed agents to monitor a person's Internet usage at a library. Casinos and Internet service providers were also asked to turn over information about customers. In the wake of the Patriot Act, eight states and hundreds of communities passed resolutions condemning the Patriot Act for violating civil liberties.

Those who support the Patriot Act point out that some tightening of the law is necessary to protect Americans from future terrorist attacks. When news of secret government wiretappings and e-mail monitoring

The US VISIT Program

In January 2004, the Homeland Security Department introduced the US VISIT program. The name is an acronym for United States Visitor and Immigrant Status Indicator Technology. Under US VISIT, all people visiting the United States from a foreign country are required to have passports with digital photos. When arriving in the United States for the first time, visitors are photographed and their fingerprints are scanned. On any future visits, their new information can be compared with the original photos and fingerscans. The procedure prevents people from using stolen or duplicate passports and other documents. Recently, US VISIT began testing a special machine that can identify foreign travelers by a special tag they carry. Information on the tag—the person's name, vital statistics, and country of origin—is transmitted to the machine via radio waves. Just as a grocery machine scans products' barcodes, the new machine is able to identify people as they enter and exit the country. The identifying information can then be accessed by workers at airports and other ports of entry into the United States.

What's in a Name?

"USA Patriot Act" is really the acronym for a much longer title: the Uniting and Strengthening America by Providing Appropriate Tools Required to Intercept and Obstruct Terrorism Act.

was revealed in late 2005, many Americans defended President Bush, arguing that the innocent have nothing to fear. Some pointed out that the **monitoring** of would-be terrorists under the Patriot Act has prevented other attacks on U.S. soil. In 2002, for example, federal agents eavesdropping on cell phones may have foiled a possible terrorist plot to attack the Brooklyn Bridge. A terrorist, after being arrested, later admitted that he had planned to take down the New York landmark. In November 2005, President Bush stated that ten terrorist acts had been prevented. In March 2006, Congress renewed the Patriot Act, with a few changes.

▲ *In September 2003, demonstrators protested the Patriot Act in Buffalo, New York, outside a facility where U.S. attorney general John Ashcroft was speaking before New York law enforcement officials.*

Making Flights Safer

On September 11, all nineteen hijackers were able to pass through airline security without any problems at all. It was clear that the United States needed better airline safety procedures. In November 2001, Congress created the Transportation Security Administration (TSA) to oversee travel safety. The law called for hiring federal agents to more carefully inspect carry-on and checked luggage before flights.

The new law also required airlines to place video monitors in the cockpit, allowing the flight crew to see what is happening in the rest of the plane, and to strengthen cockpit doors, making them more difficult for hijackers to break down. The law also allowed pilots to carry guns on board, with special permission.

One of the controversial measures taken to improve flight safety was an FAA requirement that all airport workers had to be U.S. citizens. In December 2001, in a sweep of airports across the nation, called Operation Tarmac, more than a thousand undocumented airport workers were arrested and deported.

CHAPTER 6

Taking On Saddam

O n January 29, 2002, President Bush appeared before Congress to deliver his State of the Union address. He talked about the struggle between terror and democracy in stark, black-and-white terms. He called the nations of North Korea, Iran, and Iraq the "axis of evil." Of the three countries, his harshest criticism was saved for Iraq. "This is a regime that has something to hide from the civilized world," the president said. Bush was preparing the people of the United States for war.

▼ *A map of Iraq after Operation Desert Storm illustrates the sites where weapons of mass destruction were alleged to have been produced. It had been hoped that these sites would have been destroyed during the Gulf War, but U.S. officials could not be sure that they were.*

Weapons Inspections

Under the terms of the peace treaty that ended the Persian Gulf War, Iraq had agreed to allow UN weapons inspectors into the country. Saddam Hussein, however, wanted the inspections on his own terms. At times, Saddam expelled U.S. inspectors, accusing them of

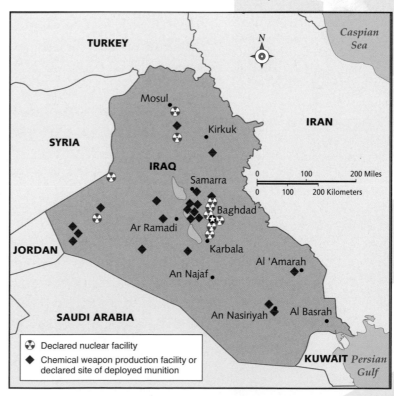

TURKEY

SYRIA

IRAQ

Mosul

Kirkuk

IRAN

Samarra

Baghdad

Ar Ramadi

Karbala

JORDAN

Al 'Amarah

An Najaf

SAUDI ARABIA

An Nasiriyah

Al Basrah

KUWAIT *Persian Gulf*

Caspian Sea

N

0   100   200 Miles
0   100   200 Kilometers

☢ Declared nuclear facility

◆ Chemical weapon production facility or declared site of deployed munition

spying. He also refused to let inspectors visit certain palaces and other key locations. Unable to complete their inspections, international weapons inspectors told the UN that Saddam was not cooperating.

By October 2002, U.S. officials were frustrated. That month, Congress authorized the president to use force against Iraq if Saddam refused to comply with the weapons inspectors. A month later, a UN inspection team returned to Iraq for the first time in four years. After its inspection, the UN team announced in January 2003 that it had found no sign of nuclear weapons, although other types of dangerous weapons were found, while others were missing and not accounted for. The team also reported that Saddam was not fully cooperating.

On February 5, Secretary of State Colin Powell asked the UN for its support in an attack on Iraq. He showed all the intelligence that the United States had collected on the weapons in Iraq. At this time, CIA believed that Saddam had chemical and biological weapons and that he was developing nuclear weapons. The CIA also believed that he intended to use some of these weapons to destroy Israel. Powell also presented evidence that seemed to tie Saddam to terrorist networks, especially al-Qaeda.

Although Bush had the sympathy of the world in the aftermath of the September 11 attacks, he now began to lose some of it. Many world leaders did not agree with Bush's plan of invading Iraq. France, Germany, and Russia, for example, wanted to give the weapons inspectors more time in Iraq. Bush was also losing some of the support of the American people for military action. While 82 percent had supported attacking Afghanistan, only 68 percent supported attacking Iraq.

Fast Fact

On January 27, 2003, the chief UN weapons inspector, Hans Blix, charged Saddam with not cooperating. He said, "Resolution 687 in 1991 …required cooperation by Iraq, but such was often withheld or given grudgingly. … Iraq appears not to have come to a genuine acceptance, not even today, of the disarmament which was demanded of it and which it needs to carry out to win the confidence of the world and to live in peace."

With or without international support, President Bush decided to take action in Iraq. On March 17, Bush gave Saddam forty-eight hours to leave Iraq. Saddam refused. Exactly two days later, the president ordered the invasion of Iraq to begin. No formal declaration of war was ever given by Congress.

A small number of nations supported Bush's decision to attack Iraq. This coalition of nations included Great Britain, Spain, Italy, Australia, and Japan. They sent troops and supplies to assist in the effort. Bush called these nations the "coalition of the willing." The main force behind the assault, however, was the United States. Seven out of eight soldiers waiting for the call to battle were American, a total of almost 250,000.

▼ *Upon liberation of Baghdad in April 2003, U.S. soldiers help Iraqi citizens topple a statue of their former leader, Saddam Hussein.*

Operation Iraqi Freedom

The first attack of Operation Iraqi Freedom began on March 20, 2003. Two air strikes targeted Saddam and members of his government in Baghdad, but failed to harm the Iraqi leader. These aerial attacks were called the "shock and awe" campaign. During the initial phase of the conflict, coalition forces flew more than six hundred bombing missions each day.

Soon after the attacks started, ground forces set off from Kuwait on a march toward Iraq's capital. As American troops marched into

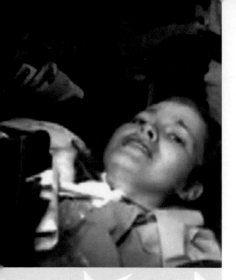

southern Iraq, they were prepared for a furious counterattack by Iraqi forces. At first, resistance was light. As the troops neared the capital, however, the fighting became much fiercer. In addition, a sandstorm slowed progress.

Meanwhile, U.S. paratroopers parachuted into the northern part of Iraq and joined with Kurdish forces for an assault on Iraq's troops and cities in the north. The troops were successful in defeating Iraq's soldiers in the region.

On April 5, American tanks entered Baghdad. After four days of fighting, the capital was captured by coalition forces. U.S. troops toppled a large statue of Saddam Hussein and replaced it with an American flag. Saddam's dictatorship was at an end, but he was still on the loose.

Capturing Saddam

With Baghdad under control, the coalition now turned its attention to conquering cities that were most loyal to Saddam. On April 14, U.S. troops took Tikrit, Saddam's birthplace and one of the areas most loyal to him. The general in charge of Iraq's temporary military government began meeting with members of the community to establish a civilian government.

On May 1, 2003, President Bush was flown to the USS *Abraham Lincoln,* a warship sailing off the coast of California. From the ship's flight deck, the president said that "major combat operations in Iraq have ended.... The transition from dictatorship to democracy will take time, but it is worth every effort." This transition proved harder than many believed it would when it was begun.

In this early phase of the conflict, 140 U.S. troops were killed, and six hundred more wounded. More than thirty British soldiers also died. The toll on the

Conflicts in Iraq and Afghanistan

Iraqi side was much higher. Although the U.S. Army was reluctant to place a figure on the number of Iraqi troops killed, some experts estimate that as many as 30,000 died. In addition, at least 3,200 Iraqi civilians were recorded as being killed in the fighting, most of them in Baghdad. Researchers in Iraq believe that many more died.

In the summer of 2003, U.S. forces began closing in on Saddam. In July, Uday and Qusay Hussein, the former leader's sons, were killed in a gunfight in Mosul, a city in northern Iraq. The two brothers were dangerous and violent men who had held important posts in their father's government. Then, in December, Saddam himself was captured while hiding in a "spider hole," a tiny hideout dug into the ground. The hole was just miles away from his hometown of Tikrit, where searchers had been looking for him for months.

Many Americans believed that the capture of Saddam would end the Iraqi resistance to coalition forces. Unfortunately, this assumption was far from the reality. In fact, for both Americans and Iraqis, the bloodiest months of war were yet to come.

▼ *An image released by the U.S. Army in December 2005 shows where Saddam Hussein was found in the town of Ad Dwara, which is outside of Tikrit, north of Baghdad.*

Farm House 1

Hut where Saddam was hiding in ground

Farm House 2

CHAPTER 7

The Conflict Continues

With Saddam now safely in coalition custody, the U.S. continued its work of bringing a democratic government to Iraq. Ongoing violence in the region made this a difficult and dangerous task. Throughout Iraq, **insurgents** continued to wage war against coalition forces. They used the familiar tools of terrorists: roadside bombings, terrorist attacks, and the kidnapping of foreign journalists and aid workers.

From May 2003 to the end of June 2004, more than eight hundred coalition troops died in Iraq. More than seven hundred of these fatalities were American troops. The death toll for Iraqi civilians continued to grow, too. Thousands of people were killed. A favorite target

▼ *The countries of Iraq and Afghanistan, with their young democracies and strong insurgent forces, continue to be a high military and diplomatic priority for the United States.*

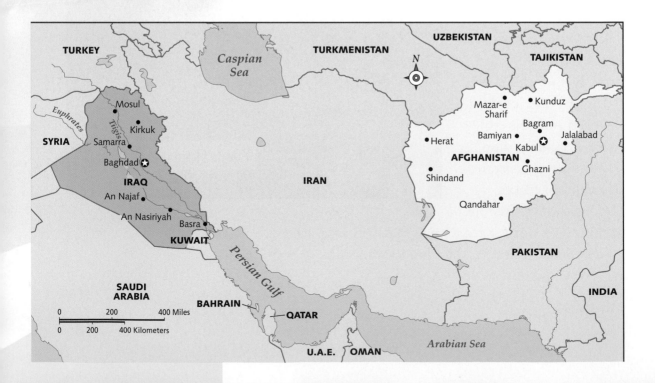

for insurgents was the newly formed Iraqi police and security forces. This was the bloodiest period of the Iraqi conflict.

As the violence continued, many people in Iraq and around the world called for the coalition forces to get out of Iraq. In late April 2004, U.S. soldiers were accused of abusing Iraqi prisoners at the Abu Ghraib prison. Appalled antiwar protesters and civil rights activists demanded punishment for the Americans involved. The incident was a black eye for the U.S. efforts to bring democracy and justice to Iraq.

On June 28, 2004, the United States transferred sovereignty, or self-rule, back into the hands of the Iraqi people. Seven months later, the country held its first democratic elections since the war. Voters waited in line for hours, even risking potential terrorist violence, to cast their votes for the 275-member Transitional National Assembly. More than half of all Iraqis who were eligible to vote did so. At the end of 2005, Iraq held a second election, this time to elect a permanent assembly.

Iraq's present government is in charge of trying Saddam Hussein and members of his political party for human rights abuses including **genocide**, war crimes, and crimes against humanity during his regime. In the first phase of Saddam's trial, prosecutors have assembled evidence to begin trying defendants for the murder of 148 people in 1982. This portion of the proceedings began in October 2005 and still continues. The trial began in Baghdad in October 2005. Prosecution witnesses described beatings, torture, and murders that took place under the former Iraqi dictator's government. Later, Saddam will be tried for **genocide** in connection with the 1988 chemical attacks that killed as many as 100,000 Kurds. The Iraqi Governing Council hopes to find the evidence

"We Were Almost All Wrong"

In October 2004, Charles A. Duelfer, the chief U.S. weapons inspector in Iraq, presented a report to Congress. Duelfer's report stated that inspectors found no WMD in Iraq and no signs of efforts to restart WMD programs. Many people accused the Bush administration of knowing that the information it had received about Iraq's possession of WMD in the months before going to war was faulty. These same critics believe that President Bush decided to go to war anyway, a charge that government officials strongly denied. Duelfer's report did go on to say, however, that Saddam would have likely resumed his quest for WMDs once UN sanctions against Iraq had been lifted.

A Veteran Returns Home

Ben Hetrick was twenty years old when his Army National Guard unit was called up for action in Iraq in 2004. He spent his twenty-first birthday working at a military hospital outside of Tikrit, a dangerous area of Iraq. After eight months of treating wounded soldiers and civilians, Hetrick returned home to his family and friends in Portland, Connecticut. In 2006, he looked back on his homecoming:

I was surprised at how many people came up to me to tell me that they "really understand what's going on." No one really knows without going there. I really don't talk about it... with my friends and family.

It wasn't really too hard to resume my normal life when I got home. But I am still extremely jumpy at times. For example, the day after I came home, I woke up to the construction crews blasting the bedrock behind our house. I thought I was under a mortar attack!

I do think about Iraq occasionally. I usually just force it out of my consciousness, though. There was a lot of stuff I really would never want to see again. I'm proud that I was able to help people whenever I could....

needed to charge Saddam with many more crimes against humanity in the future. Saddam refuses to acknowledge the right of the court to try him and insists that he is still Iraq's leader.

No End in Sight

On March 20, 2006, the third anniversary of the U.S.-led invasion, there was no end in sight to the fighting in Iraq. That day began with several roadside bombings that killed seven Iraqi police officers and the discovery of fifteen bullet-riddled bodies—including that of a thirteen-year-old girl—in Baghdad. The attacks were the work of insurgents who hope to intimidate other Iraqis into not cooperating with coalition forces and disrupting the new government. In other parts of the world, thousands of people marked the anniversary with antiwar and anti-U.S. protests.

Just days before, the Iraqi Assembly had met for the first time to begin the process of bringing the various factions in the violence-torn country together, with little success. In the early months of 2006, many observers believed the country was moving closer to a full-scale civil war between its different factions.

The first three years of the war cost the United States about $200 billion and the lives of more than twenty-three hundred soldiers. Since the war began, about one million American men and women have served in Iraq. About two-thirds of the nation's reservists have served. In March 2006, there were about 160,000 troops in Iraq. Despite a recent push in Congress to withdraw U.S. troops, President Bush has announced that American soldiers will stay in Iraq at least through 2008.

Since the beginning of the war, civilians have suffered the most. In April 2006, Iraqi Body Count, an online tally by British researchers of civilian deaths

Conflicts in Iraq and Afghanistan

in Iraq, put the death toll at more than thirty-four thousand people. This figure is close to President Bush's estimate of thirty thousand, given in December 2005. Other sources say that these numbers are too low.

In the early months of 2006, violent attacks continued daily. An official congressional report stated that in January 2006, Iraqi insurgents averaged seventy attacks per day. This was a decline from a high of ninety-nine per day in October 2005.

The economic toll on the country has also been high. Iraq's infrastructure has been destroyed. Roads, buildings, electrical lines, and water and sewage systems were damaged or destroyed in many areas. All these repairs are going to cost billions of dollars, which U.S. officials are increasingly unwilling to supply. In 2005, aid to repair the country was drastically cut by Congress.

Much of the anger and despair felt by the Iraqi people is blamed on the U.S. troops. A poll taken in October 2005 by Great Britain's Ministry of Defense found that eight out of ten Iraqis wanted foreign troops out of their country. Said one Iraqi on the third anniversary of the war, "Despite all [Saddam] did that was bad, we did not suffer as we are now. Now we have lost everything, even a sense of living."

The presence of U.S. troops has also served as a magnet for extremist and terrorist groups across the Middle East. In Iraq, they have found a war zone where they can battle the United States and its supporters. As long as groups like al-Qaeda in Iraq are active in the country the attacks on U.S. soldiers and civilians will continue.

▲ *Iraqi demonstrators who oppose the U.S. occupation of their country call for an end to foreign forces in Iraq outside the Abu-Hanifa mosque in Baghdad in April 2003.*

CHAPTER 8

The Future of American Wars

▼ Terrorist attacks occur all over the world. This photo, taken on March 11, 2004, shows the rubble of a passenger train in Madrid, Spain, destroyed by a bomb planted by a terrorist linked to al-Qaeda. The attack killed more than 191 people and injured 1,200 others.

Terrorism is a worldwide problem. On March 11, 2004, ten bombs exploded on trains in Madrid, Spain, killing 191 people. Al-Qaeda was linked to the attacks. One of the most recent attacks took place in November 2005. Three American hotels in Jordan were bombed, killing fifty-seven people. Al-Qaeda claimed responsibility.

In a report released in February 2006, the Defense Intelligence Agency stated that terrorism is still the largest threat to national security. Terrorist groups continue to be active in Iraq, Afghanistan, Lebanon, and Colombia.

As people around the world become more dependent upon computer technology, they may become vulnerable to new forms of attack. Terrorists could hack into national computer systems and retrieve sensitive documents related to national security. Enemy forces might also try to disrupt military technology in the field by blocking or changing electronic commands. Finally, terrorists could attack a nation's infrastructure by disabling computers that control banking, electricity, communications, and other aspects of everyday existence. Terrorist groups presently use the Internet to spread their message of hate and anti-Americanism.

Global Hot Spots

Terrorism is not the only threat to U.S. security and world peace. Some nations are unstable or are openly hostile to the United States and its interests abroad. Global hot spots with which the U.S. may one day see armed conflict include:

North Korea. In 2005, the communist nation of North Korea was believed to be pursuing a nuclear weapons program. Although in September 2005 the nation pledged to give up all nuclear weapons programs, it will probably not do so. North Korea also has ballistic missiles, missiles that are aimed before being fired and cannot be guided during flight to a target.

Iran. Like North Korea, Iran is also believed to be pursuing nuclear weapons. It may also have biological and chemical weapons. Iran, whose president has said he would like to destroy Israel, currently has ballistic missiles that are powerful enough to strike Israel. Iran is trying to acquire even more powerful ones. The Iranian government hates the United States for its support of Israel and interference in Iran and other parts of the Middle East, and it has worked with Iraqi rebels against coalition forces in Iraq. Iran also supports other terrorist networks in other countries in the Middle East.

U.S. diplomacy could also become important in managing conflict in:

Syria. Once known to sponsor terrorists, Syria may presently have biological weapons. Many terrorists are currently thought to be allowed to pass through the country on their way to battle coalition forces in Iraq. Also, many former Saddam supporters have found a safe haven there.

India and **Pakistan.** These neighboring states, although on good terms with the United States, have

Fast Fact

Since the end of the Korean War (1950–1953), North Korea and South Korea have existed in a state of ongoing tension. Troops from both nations still constantly patrol the neutral zone that separates the two former enemies. And while the South flourishes economically, North Korea has suffered from poverty and famine. Communist leaders in the north hope to use the threat of nuclear weapons to convince world leaders to lift economic sanctions against their country.

a bitter history and are both building up a stockpile of nuclear weapons. Both are also testing powerful ballistic missiles. Both countries have sold weapons around the world.

Russia. Russia continues to shore up its weak economy by selling submarines, aircraft, communications and radar systems, and missiles and other weapons to unstable nations.

Are We Winning?

In November 2005, members of the 9/11 Commission released a report that graded how well the U.S. government had responded to its recommendations. The commission reported that the president and Congress had made "insufficient progress" in most areas. Commission members criticized the government for not working harder to accomplish the most important goal: keeping WMDs out of the hands of terrorists. The commission also faulted the government for failing to create an alliance with other nations to address other terrorism issues.

In February 2006, President Bush spoke to National Guard members in Washington, D.C. He said that the United States and its partners were bringing positive change to Afghanistan, Iraq, and other areas of the world. U.S. and coalition actions, he said, had broken up terrorist networks across the world and disrupted plots that would have taken American lives. "The rise of freedom is leading millions to reject the dark ideology of the terrorists— and laying the foundation of peace for generations to come," Bush said. Later, he asserted that the United States is winning the war on terror.

Most Americans do not agree with the president, however. A poll taken in April 2006 indicated that

Conflicts in Iraq and Afghanistan

only about four out of ten people believed that the United States is winning the war on terrorism. Three out of ten thought that the terrorists are winning. In the same poll, nearly half of those asked said they thought the war in Iraq would, in the long run, be seen as a failure.

As Americans lose faith in U.S. efforts against terrorism and grow tired of being at war, more people are beginning to favor withdrawing troops from Iraq soon. Politicians are getting the message: In March 2006, the U.S. House of Representatives adopted an amendment that barred the establishment of permanent bases in Iraq.

Some Americans fear that President Bush is preparing to take the United States to war again, this time against Iran. In the spring of 2006, Iran was poised to defy a UN deadline to stop enriching uranium, a step toward making nuclear weapons. The Bush administration has said that "all options are on the table," meaning that the threat of warfare has not been ruled out.

As support for Bush at home erodes, anti-American sentiment increases. Many nations did not support the coalition invasion of Iraq and now criticize ongoing U.S. efforts there. Few would likely welcome a U.S. attack on Iran. Bush and other top officials, however, believe that the United States must continue to play a leadership role in spreading democracy. Said Bush, "Every step toward freedom in the world makes this country safer—so across the world the United States of America is acting boldly in freedom's cause."

▲ One of the global hot spots in the Middle East is Iran, which is pursuing a nuclear program in spite of warnings from the International Atomic Energy Agency (IAEA) and Western countries. An Iranian woman, pictured here in January 2006, shooting at a target, is among the thousands of citizens who favor Iran's decision to ignore the United States' protests, believing that U.S. influence is unwelcome in Iran.

TIME LINE

1979	Saddam Hussein comes to power in Iraq.
1988	Muslim extremists form the terrorist organization al-Qaeda in Afghanistan.
1990	Saddam invades Kuwait; the UN imposes economic sanctions on Iraq.
1991	January: A international coalition of troops, led by the United States, begins war against Iraq; February: President George H. W. Bush declares a cease-fire; April: as part of the peace agreement to end the Persian Gulf War, Saddam agrees to destroy all WMDs.
1993	February: Terrorists set off a bomb in the parking garage of the World Trade Center in New York City; June: President Bill Clinton launches air strikes against Iraq in retaliation for a failed assassination attempt on former President Bush.
1996	The United States launches missile strikes against Iraq after Saddam orders an attack on a Kurdish town.
1998	August: Terrorists attack two American embassies in Africa, killing more than 230 people; December: Clinton launches Operation Desert Fox to destroy Iraqi weapons-making sites; U.S. air strikes target al-Qaeda training camps in Afghanistan.
2000	Suicide bombers attack the USS *Cole.*
2001	September: Terrorists attack targets in New York and Washington, D.C., causing the deaths of almost 3,000 Americans; October: the United States and other nations begin Operation Enduring Freedom to find Osama bin Laden and end terrorism in Afghanistan; the Office of Homeland Security is created; Congress passes the Patriot Act; November: Congress creates the Transportation Security Administration.
2002	October: Congress authorizes the president to use force if Saddam continues to defy weapons inspectors; November: Congress establishes the 9/11 Commission.
2003	February: The United States asks the UN for international support in an attack on Iraq; March: President George W. Bush orders the invasion of Iraq; May: President Bush announces the end of major combat operations in Iraq; July: Saddam's two sons are killed; December: Saddam is captured by U.S. troops.
2004	April: The United States is accused of abusing prisoners at Abu Ghraib prison; June: The United States transfers sovereignty of Iraq back to the Iraqi people; July: The 9/11 Commission reports that the terrorist attacks might have been prevented; new construction on the World Trade Center site begins; October: A CIA report states that Iraq did not have WMDs.
2005	January: Iraqis take part in their first democratic elections since the war; October: The first of Saddam's trials begins in Iraq.
2006	March: Congress renews the Patriot Act; June: Abu Masab al-Zarqawi, leader of al-Qaeda in Iraq, is killed by U.S. air strike.

GLOSSARY

aerial by means of aircraft

anthrax a type of bacteria that occurs naturally in both wild and domestic animals

cells branches of a terrorist network

coalition an alliance, usually temporary, of people or nations

debris scattered remains of something destroyed

deploying putting troops in a ready position for combat

economic sanctions punishments imposed on a nation to force it to comply with international law

fatwa a decree issued by a Muslim who specializes in religious law

genocide the systematic killing of a cultural or racial group

Gulf War syndrome a medical condition affecting some veterans of the Gulf War causing headaches, joint pain, dizziness, and breathing problems

insurgents rebel fighters

intelligence information or knowledge about an enemy that is gained through secret operations

Islam a religion centered on the teachings of the Prophet Muhammad (c. A.D. 570–632)

Islamist radicals people who advocate Islamic government and, often the use of violence in support of their views

Kurdish relating to the Kurd's language or culture

liberate to set free from oppression

monitoring a person or agency that watches over, cautions, and reprimands conduct

multinational involving more than two countries

Muslims a follower of Islam

nation-building the process of restructuring a failing nation, usually undertaken by a more powerful nation

networks several terrorist groups that work together toward a common goal

reservists members of the armed forces who, although not actively serving, are available to fight in an emergency

spores single-celled bacteria capable of growing into a new organism

terrorism the use of violence to create an atmosphere of fear in an effort to bring about political change

turmoil a state of extreme upheaval

weapons of mass destruction (WMD) any weapons—nuclear, chemical, or biological—that can cause widespread death and damage

United Nations (UN) an international organization founded to promote peace, security, and economic development around the world

FOR FURTHER INFORMATION

Books

Balaghi, Shiva. *Saddam Hussein: A Biography.* Greenwood Press, 2006.

Brewer, Paul. *September 11 and Radical Islamic Terrorism (*Terrorism in Today's World*).* World Almanac Library, 2006.

Greene, Meg. *The Hunt for Osama bin Laden.* Rosen, 2005.

King, John. *Iraq Then And Now (*The Middle East*).* Raintree, 2005.

Landau, Elaine. *Osama bin Laden: A War Against the West.* Twenty-First Century, 2002.

Streissguth, Thomas. *Afghanistan (*History of Nations*).* Greenhaven Press, 2005.

Weitzman, Stanley. *Terrorism (*Global Issues*).* Walrus Books, 2006.

Zeinert, Karen and Mary Mills. *The Brave Women of the Gulf Wars: Operation Desert Storm and Operation Iraqi Freedom (*Women at War*).* Twenty-First Century Press, 2006.

Web Sites

www.cnn.com/interactive/maps/world/fullpage.troop.deployments/ world.index.html

www.pbs.org/wgbh/pages/frontline/gulf/index.html

www.historycentral.com/desert_storm/index.html

Publisher's note to educators and parents: Our editors have carefully reviewed these Web sites to ensure that they are suitable for children. Many Web sites change frequently, however, and we cannot guarantee that a site's future contents will continue to meet our high standards of quality and educational value. Be advised that children should be closely supervised whenever they access the Internet.

INDEX

About the Author

Robin Doak is a writer of fiction and nonfiction books for children, ranging from elementary to high school levels. Subjects she has written on include the human body, profiles of U.S. presidents, athletes, and American immigration. Robin is a former editor of *Weekly Reader* and, in addition to her extensive experience writing for children, has also written numerous support guides for educators. Robin holds a Bachelor of Arts degree in English, with an emphasis on journalism, from the University of Connecticut.